Heirs to the Queen of Hearts

Tracing Magical Genealogy

Prof. Oddfellow

Little acquainted with the use
Of mystic genealogy,
I often attempted to deduce
The birth of Inconsistency
—Michael Wodhull,
"Inconsistency" (1772)

Heirs to the Queen of Hearts:

Tracing Magical Genealogy

We begin because of two conditions.

First, our motor and verbal skills have developed enough for us to sit and listen to our parents.

Second, one of them sits on the floor with us and, taking one of our hands, says: "Look, these are your fingers."

–Calvin Clawson,
The Mathematical Traveler (2003)

Cicero: "Not to know what took place before one was born is to remain forever a child."

We travel back...

All the way back to the trees and caves, the route liberally sprinkled with profanities.
–William W. Johnstone, *Scream of Eagles*.

$#!†

To Know Truly Is To Know As In a Dream*

We wander, you and I, through a family of trees. We admire the majestic heights of the interweaving branches. It's as if these trees grew knowing that we'd seek them for climbing.

Yet there's more here than meets the eye. We realize, with fleeting surprise, that I'm holding a shovel and you a divining rod.

Point the way, and let's dig. Let's get to the bottom of how it all relates. Even if we've forgotten the past, it remembers us.† Even if our treasure map is pirated, there's still the thrill of the hunt. Though it may all be a dream, we can be lucid as the story unfolds, any-who.

*Kuang-Ming Wu, *The Butterfly as Companion* (1990)
† Sarah Dessen, *What Happened to Goodbye* (2011)

Owning Our Exalted Heritage

To stand upon the shoulders of the mighty requires not only a colossal step up but also concerted balancing and adjusted perspectives. What a hefty responsibility comes with owning exalted heritage. What an effort of imagination it takes to draw our birthright into the limelight so as to illuminate the missing branches in our family trees. When missing branches are of royal and/or magical origin, we find ourselves facing some rather profound questions and challenges. To what crown (or crowning glory) are we the natural successors? To what dignities? What traditions are our responsibility to keep alive? What untapped powers? If our *Weltanschauung* does not account for an Otherworld, how can we reconcile our nymph-glands? How are the descendants of an exotic deity to appease another holy ghost?

Truly, to quest for the higher echelons of human life, to scale ancestral branches, is to hang topsy-turvy with Odin on the World Tree.

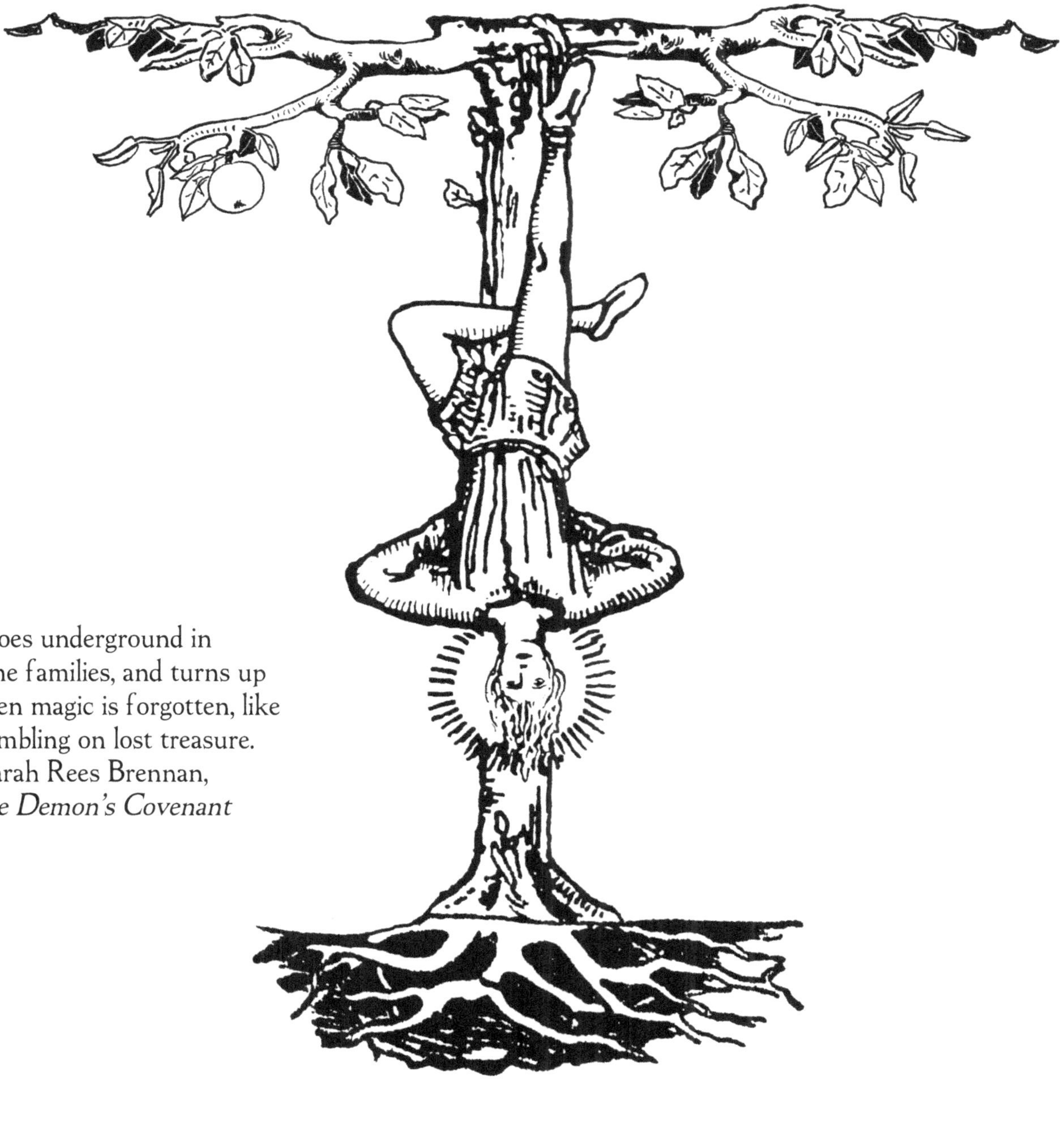

It goes underground in some families, and turns up when magic is forgotten, like stumbling on lost treasure.
–Sarah Rees Brennan,
The Demon's Covenant

Pictured: (Family) tree rings are suggestive of a radial ancestry diagram.

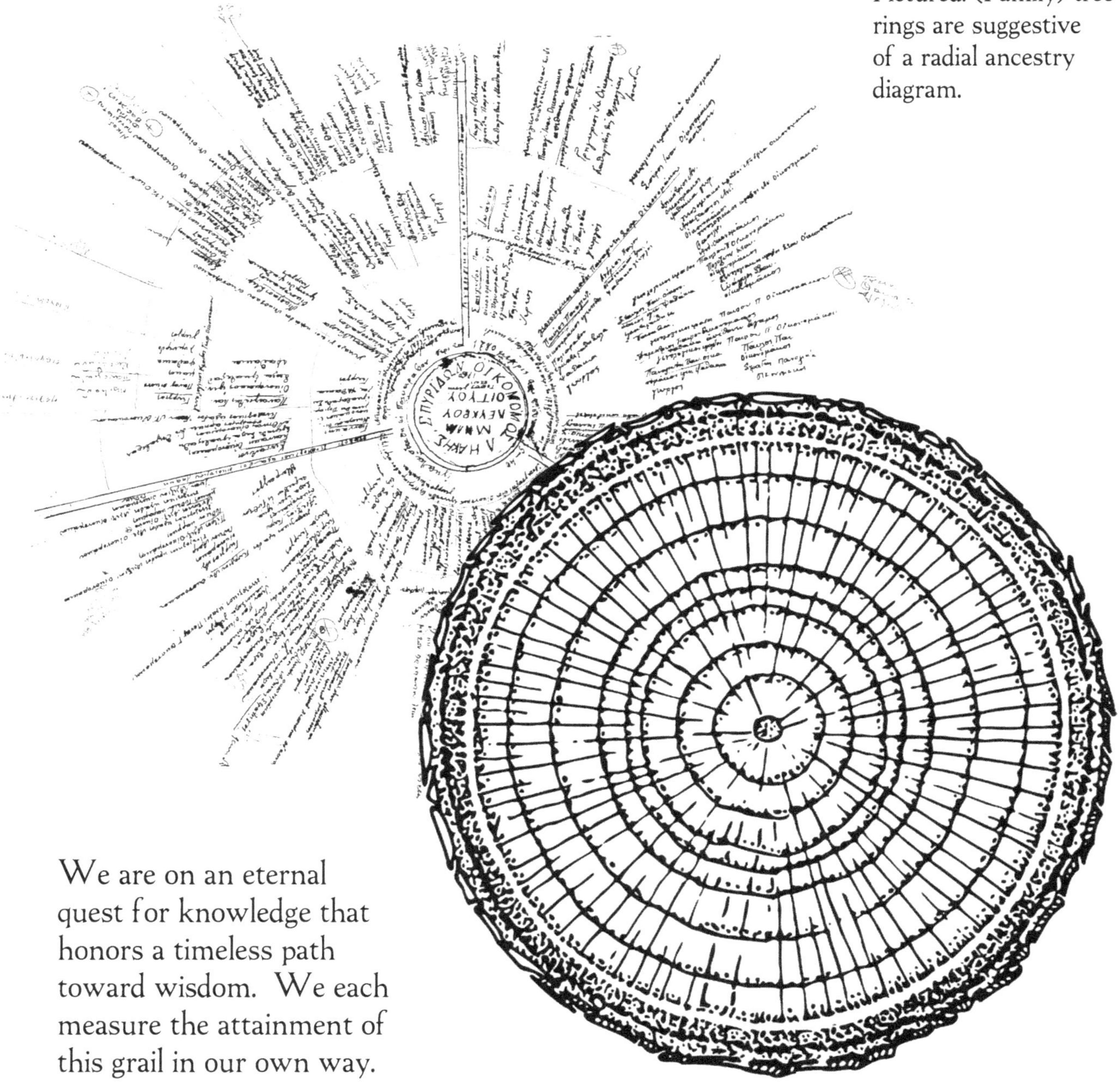

We are on an eternal quest for knowledge that honors a timeless path toward wisdom. We each measure the attainment of this grail in our own way.
–David Morehouse, *Remote Viewing*, 2008

How Climbing a Family Tree Elevates Character

Pictured: Daniel Webster

Daniel Webster: While a regard for ancestry may indeed nourish a weak pride or vanity, a philosophical respect for our ancestors elevates the character and improves the heart. "Human and mortal though we are, we are, nevertheless, not mere insulated beings, without relation to the past or future. Neither the point of time or the spot of earth in which we physically live bounds our rational and intellectual enjoyments. We live in the past by a knowledge of its history, in the future by hope and anticipation. By ascending to an association with our ancestors; by contemplating their example, and studying their character; by partaking their sentiments, and imbibing their spirit; by accompanying them in their toils; by sympathizing in their sufferings and rejoicing in their successes and triumphs,– we mingle our own existence with theirs and seem to belong to their age. We become their contemporaries, live the lives they lived, endure what they endured, and partake in the reward which they enjoyed" (*The Utah Genealogical and Historical Magazine*).

The real reason we study genealogy is because we seek what Sir William Osler called

The silent influence of character on character.

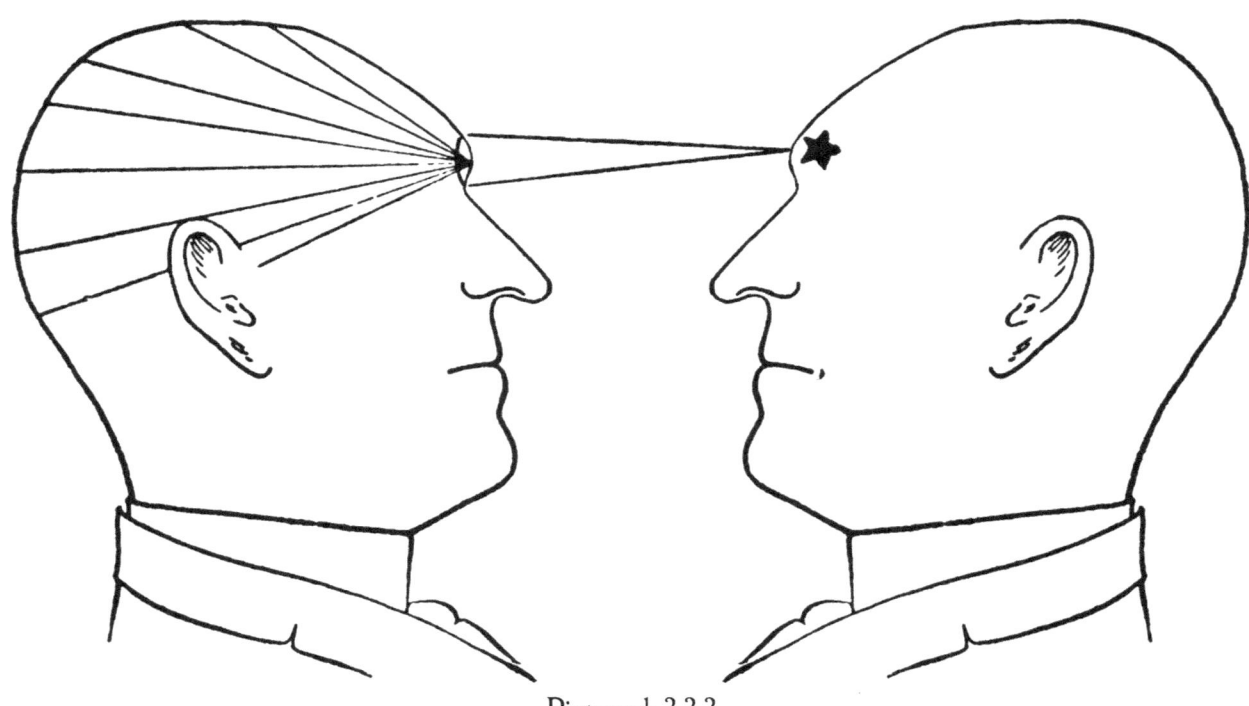

Pictured: ? ? ?

How Genealogy is Like a Card Trick

We know that a typically deceptive card trick works by introducing a set of reasonable assumptions which later prove to be false. The magician establishes the reasoning, the participant takes the assumptions for granted, and so the magician can deliver the knock out.

Similarly, genealogy "helps us to see how what we take as necessary was not always the case," as Hoy and McCarthy explain in *Critical Theory* (1994). "The point is not to show that historical forms of rationality are in fact irrational, or what an ideal form of rationality would be. Instead, the goal is to realize that because these forms of rationality have been made, they can be unmade." In other words, "genealogy analyzes practices that were instituted in the name of reason but that threaten to harden into unquestioned but oppressive necessity. The genealogical diagnosis itself implies that there is still room for thinking about the possibility of transforming these practices. Foucault puts this point succinctly . . . , suggesting that the value of genealogy is that it 'serves to show how that-which-is has not always been,' and thereby shows 'why and how that-which-is might no longer be that-which-is.'"

For Foucault, an effective genealogy is just like a magic trick in that it destroys our unquestioned assumptions about reality. Genealogy reveals the colorful mask we display for public viewing, then "cuts through this mask, only to make another discovery. Behind it there is no essential identity, no unified spirit or will, no naked subject stripped of its colorful dress. Rather, there is only a matrix of intersecting lines" (Michael Clifford, *Political Genealogy After Foucault*, 2001).

Pictured: a magician conjures the intersecting emanations of the Kabbalistic Tree of Life (Sephirot).

Honest Graft: Transplanted Pedigree

On our eternal quest for the impossible goal of knowing what it is to be human, we can't all be as lucky as Hungarian escape artist David Merlini, who inherited that wizardly name from his Italian father. Yet our pedigree need not be limited to direct bloodlines. Genealogy traces *relationships*. For example, the line connecting Jean Eugène Robert-Houdin to Erik Weisz as Houdini is a genuine relationship from the father of modern magic to a beneficiary, and it can be charted accordingly.

Parenthetically, the Houdin-Houdini line is technically a matrilineal relationship, as Houdin was the maiden name of Robert's wife.

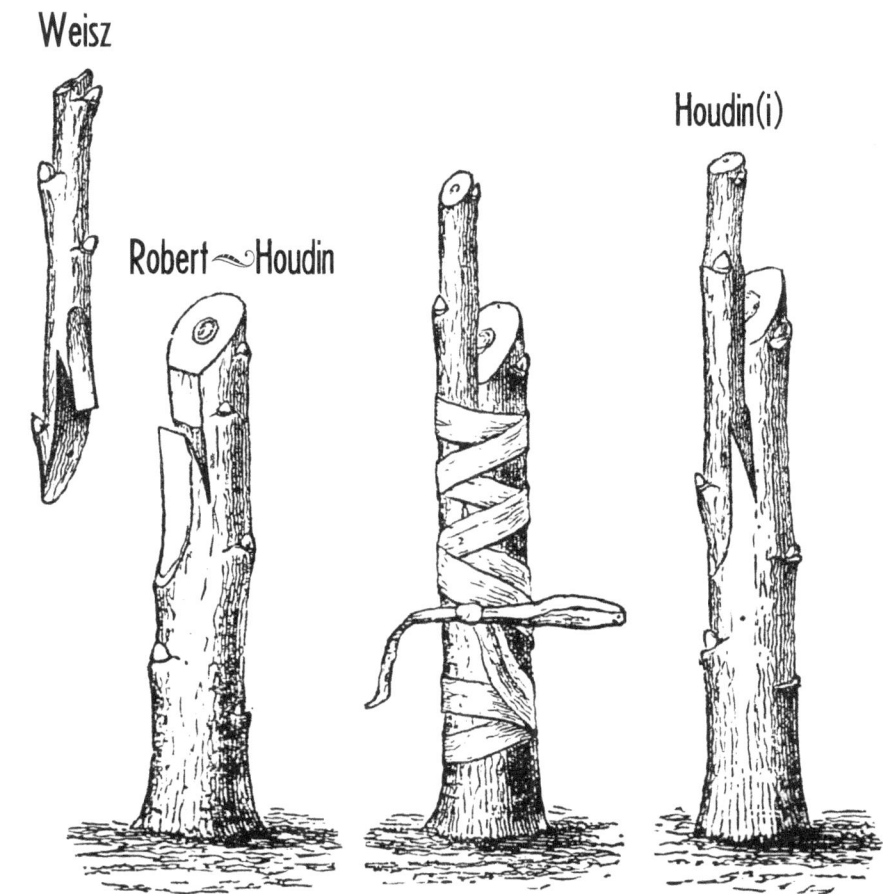

Pictured: Family tree horticulture: inserting a graft on a stock.

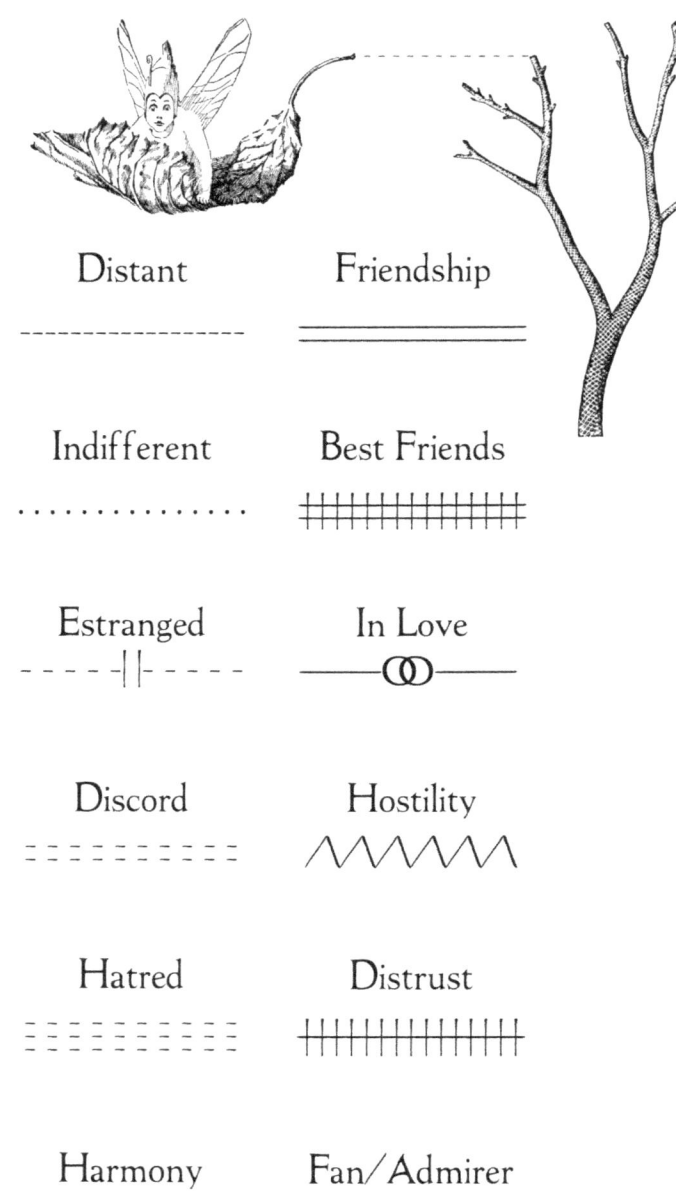

Genogram notation offers a variety of lines to define different types of familial, emotional, and social relationships. With genogram notations, a family tree can be significantly more detailed. Emily Marlin calls genograms "family trees that can talk" (*Genograms: The New Tool For Exploring the Personality, Career, and Love Patterns You Inherit*, 1989).

Distant

Friendship

Indifferent

Best Friends

Estranged

In Love

Discord

Hostility

Hatred

Distrust

Harmony

Fan/Admirer

The Art and Seance of Producing a Family Tree

SPIRITUALISM (continued)

PLAYING MEDIUM, DUNNINGER CONJURES UP SOMEBODY'S FAMILY TREE FOR A GREAT SPIRIT PHOTOGRAPH

Granted: "The art of illusion is not genetic. Having a magician in the family tree doesn't vouch for talent in the rest of the bloodline" (Carol O'Connell, *The Man Who Cast Two Shadows*, 1996). However: our fans likely don't know that.

Pictured: Joseph Dunninger in *Life*, June 16, 1941.

What are our chances of being related to Blackstone, Thurston, Kellar, or Dante? Or to a fairy queen, a Chinese immortal, a fallen angel, or a playing card? The chances increase exponentially, the farther back in time we journey. The formula for the number of ancestors in a given generation is $2^n = x$, where n is the number of generations back and x equals the number of individuals in that generation. To wit:

GENERATIONS BACK	(n)	NUMBER OF INDIVIDUALS (x)	BIRTH YEAR
self	0	1	1950
parents	1	2	1920
grandparents	2	4	1890
great-grandparents	3	8	1860
2nd great-grandparents	4	16	1830
3rd great-grandparents	5	32	1800
4th great-grandparents	6	64	1770
5th great-grandparents	7	128	1740
6th great-grandparents	8	256	1710
7th great-grandparents	9	512	1680
8th great-grandparents	10	1,024	1650
9th great-grandparents	11	2,048	1620
10th great-grandparents	12	4,096	1590
11th great-grandparents	13	8,192	1560
12th great-grandparents	14	16,384	1530
13th great-grandparents	15	32,768	1500
14th great-grandparents	16	65,536	1470
15th great-grandparents	17	131,072	1440
16th great-grandparents	18	262,144	1410
17th great-grandparents	19	524,288	1380
18th great-grandparents	20	1,048,576	1350

Going back 40 generations, any one person has a *trillion* ancestors. The key is to trace a particular path and *claim* the family line.

Untold numbers of people may be related to Elizabeth of York, the historical Queen of Hearts, but only your humble guide and confidant has avowed the honor.

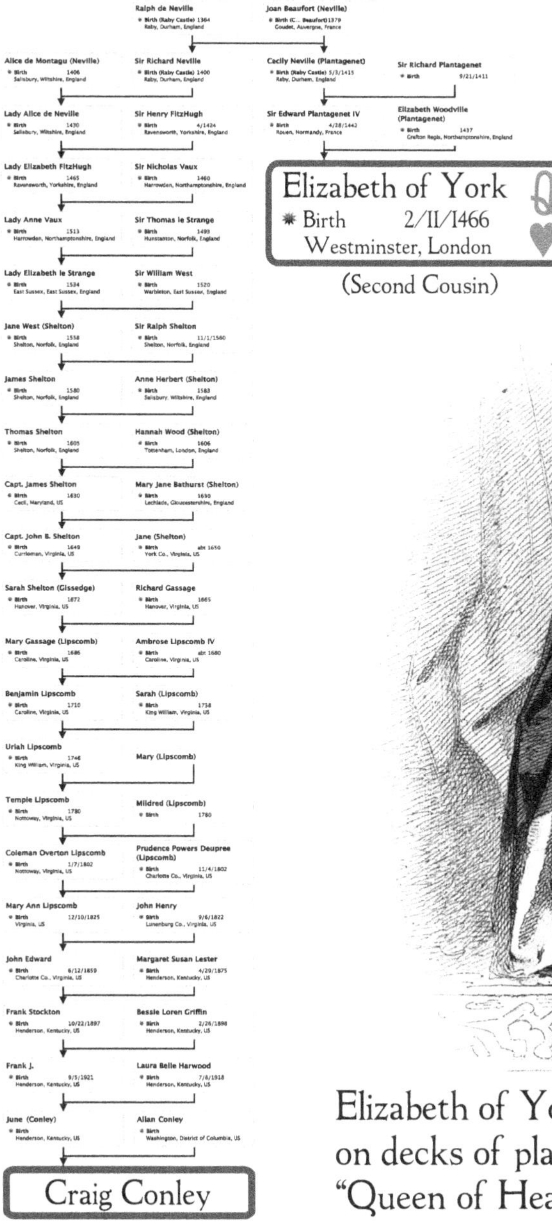

Ralph de Neville
● Birth (Raby Castle) 1364
Raby, Durham, England

Joan Beaufort (Neville)
● Birth (C... Beaufort)1379
Goudet, Auvergne, France

Alice de Montagu (Neville)
● Birth 1406
Salisbury, Wiltshire, England

Sir Richard Neville
● Birth (Raby Castle) 1400
Raby, Durham, England

Cacily Neville (Plantagenet)
● Birth (Raby Castle) 5/3/1415
Raby, Durham, England

Sir Richard Plantagenet
● Birth 9/21/1411

Lady Alice de Neville
● Birth 1430
Salisbury, Wiltshire, England

Sir Henry FitzHugh
● Birth 1424
Ravenworth, Yorkshire, England

Sir Edward Plantagenet IV
● Birth 4/28/1442
Rouen, Normandy, France

Elizabeth Woodville (Plantagenet)
● Birth 1437
Grafton Regis, Northamptonshire, England

Lady Elizabeth FitzHugh
● Birth 1465
Ravensworth, Yorkshire, England

Sir Nicholas Vaux
● Birth 1460
Harrowden, Northamptonshire, England

Elizabeth of York Q
✳ Birth   2/11/1466
Westminster, London
(Second Cousin) ♥

Lady Anne Vaux
● Birth 1513
Harrowden, Northamptonshire, England

Sir Thomas le Strange
● Birth 1493
Hunstanton, Norfolk, England

Lady Elizabeth le Strange
● Birth 1534
East Sussex, East Sussex, England

Sir William West
● Birth 1520
Warbleton, East Sussex, England

Jane West (Shelton)
● Birth 1558
Shelton, Norfolk, England

Sir Ralph Shelton
● Birth 11/1/1560
Shelton, Norfolk, England

James Shelton
● Birth 1580
Shelton, Norfolk, England

Anne Herbert (Shelton)
● Birth 1583
Salisbury, Wiltshire, England

Thomas Shelton
● Birth 1605
Shelton, Norfolk, England

Hannah Wood (Shelton)
● Birth 1606
Tottenham, London, England

Capt. James Shelton
● Birth 1630
Cecil, Maryland, US

Mary Jane Bathurst (Shelton)
● Birth 1630
Lechlade, Gloucestershire, England

Capt. John B. Shelton
● Birth 1649
Currieman, Virginia, US

Jane (Shelton)
● Birth abt 1650
York Co., Virginia, US

Sarah Shelton (Gissedge)
● Birth 1671
Hanover, Virginia, US

Richard Gassage
● Birth 1665
Hanover, Virginia, US

Mary Gassage (Lipscomb)
● Birth 1686
Caroline, Virginia, US

Ambrose Lipscomb IV
● Birth abt 1680
Caroline, Virginia, US

Benjamin Lipscomb
● Birth 1710
Caroline, Virginia, US

Sarah (Lipscomb)
● Birth 1718
King William, Virginia, US

Uriah Lipscomb
● Birth 1748
King William, Virginia, US

Mary (Lipscomb)

Temple Lipscomb
● Birth 1780
Nottoway, Virginia, US

Mildred (Lipscomb)
● Birth 1780

Coleman Overton Lipscomb
● Birth 1/7/1802
Nottoway, Virginia, US

Prudence Powers Deupree (Lipscomb)
● Birth 11/4/1802
Charlotte Co., Virginia, US

Mary Ann Lipscomb
● Birth 12/10/1825
Virginia, US

John Henry
● Birth 9/6/1822
Lunenburg Co., Virginia, US

John Edward
● Birth 6/12/1859
Charlotte Co., Virginia, US

Margaret Susan Lester
● Birth 4/29/1875
Henderson, Kentucky, US

Frank Stockton
● Birth 10/22/1897
Henderson, Kentucky, US

Bessie Loren Griffin
● Birth 2/26/1898
Henderson, Kentucky, US

Frank J.
● Birth 9/5/1921
Henderson, Kentucky, US

Laura Belle Harwood
● Birth 7/6/1918
Henderson, Kentucky, US

June (Conley)
● Birth
Henderson, Kentucky, US

Allan Conley
● Birth
Washington, District of Columbia, US

Craig Conley

Elizabeth of York, wife of Henry VII, has been immortalized on decks of playing cards throughout English History as the "Queen of Hearts," holding a Tudor Rose.

If your family includes a name below, you may be related to the Queen of Hearts!

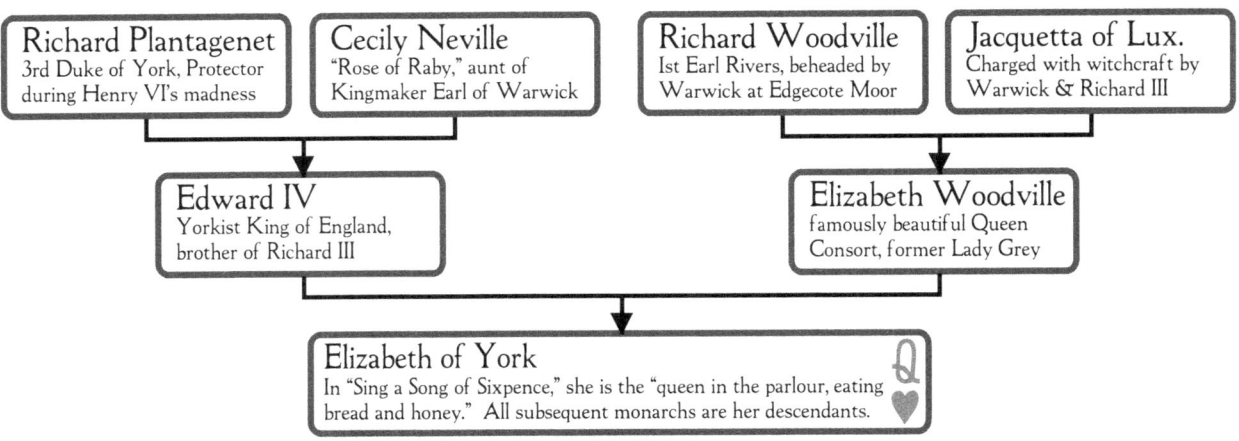

Richard Plantagenet
3rd Duke of York, Protector during Henry VI's madness

Cecily Neville
"Rose of Raby," aunt of Kingmaker Earl of Warwick

Richard Woodville
1st Earl Rivers, beheaded by Warwick at Edgecote Moor

Jacquetta of Lux.
Charged with witchcraft by Warwick & Richard III

Edward IV
Yorkist King of England, brother of Richard III

Elizabeth Woodville
famously beautiful Queen Consort, former Lady Grey

Elizabeth of York
In "Sing a Song of Sixpence," she is the "queen in the parlour, eating bread and honey." All subsequent monarchs are her descendants.

DESCENDANT FAMILY NAMES:

| Margaret Tudor | Henry VIII | Mary Tudor |
Queen of Scots	King of England	Queen of France
August, Bard, Barrett, Beauclerck, Brent, Brodie, Bruce, Brydges, Campbell, Caroline, Cockey, Cornelius, Cranston, Darnley, Dick, Dishington, Douglas, Drummond, Dyer, Erdal, Fitzroy, Fraser, Gordon, Grant, Gray, Greniffe, Grey, Guelph, Hammond, Home, Honey-man, Howard, Hughes, Iams, Innes, Kennedy, Kinloch, Lennox, Leslie, Lindsay, Mackenzie, Mackintosh, Maxwell, Moddy, Montgomerie, Moody, Mudie, Nugent, Phelps, Ridgley, Ross, Scott, Seltz, Sinclair, Stewart, Stuart, Sutherland, Tylie, Umphrey, von der Pfalz, Walker, Wemyss, Worthington, ...	Annesley, Beauchamp, Bellingham, Blount, Carey, Cheke, Chichester, Clifton, Davenport, Devereux, Digby, Dyer, Edwards, Eldred, Finch, Fitzgerald, Fitzroy, Fox, Grosvenor, Harcourt, Harris, Harrington, Howard, Humphrey, Johnson, Joyner, Knollys, Knowles, Leighton, Lippitt, Lloyd, Lort, Lower, Ludlam, Ludlow, Martin, Paget, Palmes, Parrott, Pelham, Percy, Phillips, Rich, Rodgers, Seymour, Shirley, Sidney, Smith, St. John, Stukely, Swain, Sidney, Sydney, Talbot, Thynue, Tilghman, Tillman, Vaughan, West, Winslow, Woodward, Zouche, ...	Alger, Barrett, Barton, Beauchamp, Bedingfield, Boyle, Brandon, Bridges, Bruce, Bruen, Cardigan, Cary, Cecil, Clifford, Conway, Cooper, Dilke, Douglas, Dunmore, Dyer, Egerton, Finch, Fraser, Graham, Grenville, Grey, Hall, Hastings, Herbert, Herford, Hill, Hinton, Hull, Kerr, Lascelles, Leigh, Manners, Murray, Nairne, Noel, Oliphant, Perceval, Pigott, Portman, Rich, Robertson, Robinson, Rollo, Sackville, Scott, Seymour, Shernerd, Slocum, Stanley, Stokes, Thynne, Trelawny, Tuchet, Tucker, Tufton, Vaughan, Ward, Watson, Wentworth, Wilkinson, Wrottesley, Wyndham, ...

Playing Card Personages

Glamorous as the Queen of Hearts may be, there's an entire deck of playing cards to which we might be related. On the following pages, we'll note the major historical figures associated with the face cards, as well as other playing card personages.

K ♣

Alexander the Great
King of Macedon

Q ♣

Marie of Anjou
Queen consort of King
Charles VII of France

J ♣

Lancelot
Arthur's knight,
father of Galahad

K ♦

Julius Caesar
Dictator of the Roman
Republic

Q ♦

Agnès Sorel
Mistress of Charles
VII of France

J ♦

Hector
Warrior of Troy

David
King of Judah
and Israel

Joan of Arc
French national heroine

Ogier the Dane
Charlemagne's knight,
carried off by the witch
Morgan la Fay in
Arthurian legend

Charlemagne
first Holy Roman
emperor

Elizabeth of York
mother of
King Henry VIII

La Hire
Etienne de Vignoles,
knight & hero of France

Other Playing Card Associations

King of Spades
Confederate General Robert E. Lee was
called the "King of Spades" for his excessive digging of trenches around Richmond. These trenches would later play a pivotal role in battles near the end of the war.

Queen of Spades
Russian Princess Natalia Petrovna Golitsyna presumed to be the model for the countess in short story "The Queen of Spades."

Jack of Spades
Army General John A. Logan was known as the "Jack of Spades."

Kings of Diamonds
Jewelers Charles Lewis Tiffany and Harry Winston were each dubbed "King of Diamonds."

Queen of Diamonds
Professional baseball catcher Lavonne Paire Davis was called "Queen of Diamonds."

Jack of Diamonds
Max A. Thoman, Lieutenant Colonel of the 59th New York Volunteer Infantry, was known as the "Jack of Diamonds."

King of Hearts
For his charming manner and handsome appearance, Charles Talbot, Duke of Shrewsbury, was called "the King of Hearts" by William III. Jonathan Swift dubbed Talbot "the finest gentleman we have."

Queen of Hearts
Elizabeth, Queen of Bohemia, was known as the "Queen of Hearts."

Jack of Hearts
Philadelphia police officer Jack Hart was known as "Jack of Hearts."

King of Clubs
The juggler Gus Hill was dubbed the "King of Clubs."

Queen of Clubs
Julia Ward Howe, "America's Grand Old Woman," was widely known for her "Battle Hymn of the Republic" and was affectionately called "the Queen of Clubs" in honor of her philanthropic work.

Jack of Clubs
Arizona gunfighter Jack Brenen was called the "Jack of Clubs" for reasons now forgotten.

Guiding Spirits of the Deck

Here's a challenge for romantics, mystics, or otherwise poetical-minded magi: trace the *guiding spirits* of the playing cards. For example, the Ace of Hearts' guiding spirit is the Scarlet Hunter of Native American lore. He comes from the legendary White Valley, the Place of Peace, where the sleepers are. He is known as the Sentinel of the North and the Lover of the Lost. If you have indigenous American heritage and

THEN PIERRE WITH A LITTLE WEIRD LAUGH REACHED OUT AND TURNED OVER—THE ACE OF HEARTS.

your ancestral line reaches a mysterious dead end in the hills of the far north, you may be related to the Scarlet Hunter/Ace of Hearts.

THEN THE SCARLET HUNTER SPOKE.

A game of "whoever draws the Ace of Hearts, wins" conjures the sentinel of legend, the Scarlet Hunter. From *The English Illustrated* magazine, 1894.

Six Generations of the Magical Bamberg Dynasty

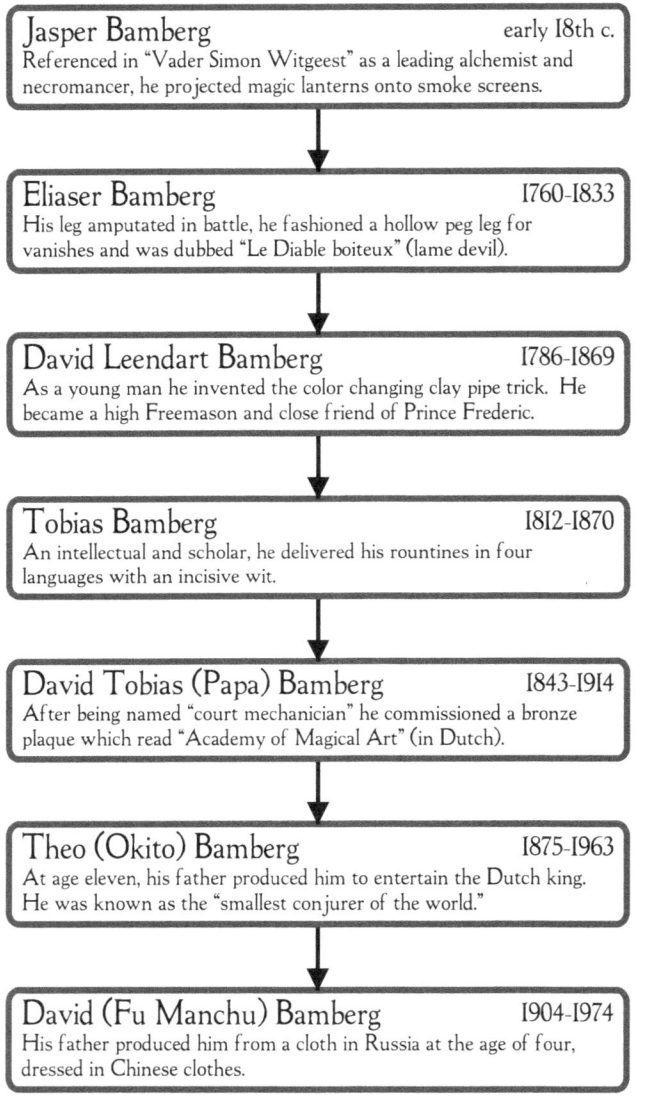

Jasper Bamberg — early 18th c.
Referenced in "Vader Simon Witgeest" as a leading alchemist and necromancer, he projected magic lanterns onto smoke screens.

Eliaser Bamberg — 1760-1833
His leg amputated in battle, he fashioned a hollow peg leg for vanishes and was dubbed "Le Diable boiteux" (lame devil).

David Leendart Bamberg — 1786-1869
As a young man he invented the color changing clay pipe trick. He became a high Freemason and close friend of Prince Frederic.

Tobias Bamberg — 1812-1870
An intellectual and scholar, he delivered his rountines in four languages with an incisive wit.

David Tobias (Papa) Bamberg — 1843-1914
After being named "court mechanician" he commissioned a bronze plaque which read "Academy of Magical Art" (in Dutch).

Theo (Okito) Bamberg — 1875-1963
At age eleven, his father produced him to entertain the Dutch king. He was known as the "smallest conjurer of the world."

David (Fu Manchu) Bamberg — 1904-1974
His father produced him from a cloth in Russia at the age of four, dressed in Chinese clothes.

Bamberg's fame sounds yet in those days:
Father gave the art to his son.
At the market is shown the first of the
　　Bambergs of this name and art.
But whatever you may admire,
It is only magic—nothing more.
Witchcraft it never was,
And bewitchment is what you see.
—David Bamberg, *Illusion Show* (1988)

DESCENDANT NAMES
OF KNOWN COMMON
ANCESTORS:

Abraham
Cohen
Delden
Drilsma
Hamburger
Kinsbergen
Levie
Schrijver
Simons
Spraakmeester
. . .

The Thurston Family Tree
(An exclusive of your humble guide and confidant)

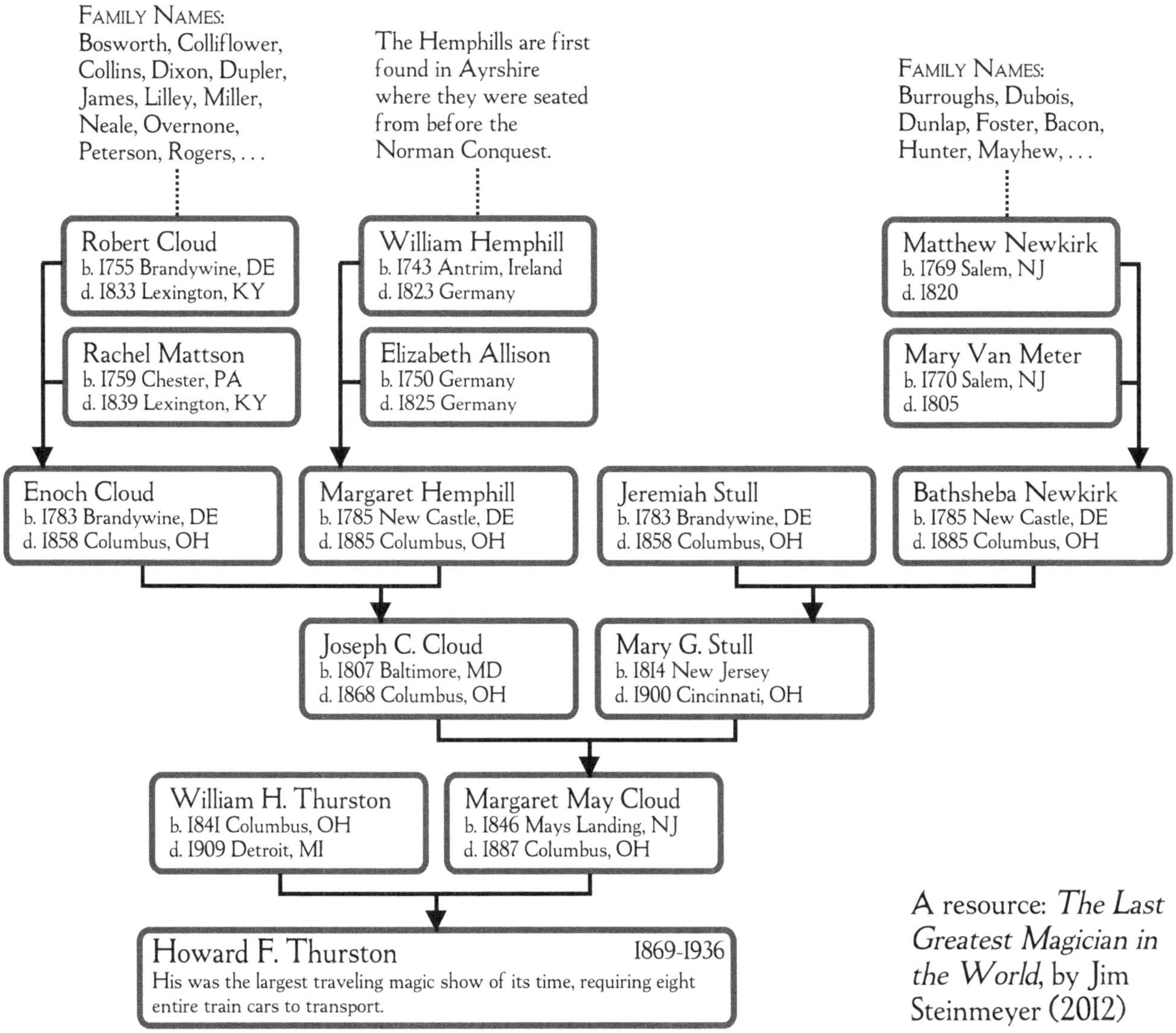

FAMILY NAMES:
Bosworth, Colliflower,
Collins, Dixon, Dupler,
James, Lilley, Miller,
Neale, Overnone,
Peterson, Rogers, . . .

The Hemphills are first
found in Ayrshire
where they were seated
from before the
Norman Conquest.

FAMILY NAMES:
Burroughs, Dubois,
Dunlap, Foster, Bacon,
Hunter, Mayhew, . . .

Robert Cloud
b. 1755 Brandywine, DE
d. 1833 Lexington, KY

William Hemphill
b. 1743 Antrim, Ireland
d. 1823 Germany

Matthew Newkirk
b. 1769 Salem, NJ
d. 1820

Rachel Mattson
b. 1759 Chester, PA
d. 1839 Lexington, KY

Elizabeth Allison
b. 1750 Germany
d. 1825 Germany

Mary Van Meter
b. 1770 Salem, NJ
d. 1805

Enoch Cloud
b. 1783 Brandywine, DE
d. 1858 Columbus, OH

Margaret Hemphill
b. 1785 New Castle, DE
d. 1885 Columbus, OH

Jeremiah Stull
b. 1783 Brandywine, DE
d. 1858 Columbus, OH

Bathsheba Newkirk
b. 1785 New Castle, DE
d. 1885 Columbus, OH

Joseph C. Cloud
b. 1807 Baltimore, MD
d. 1868 Columbus, OH

Mary G. Stull
b. 1814 New Jersey
d. 1900 Cincinnati, OH

William H. Thurston
b. 1841 Columbus, OH
d. 1909 Detroit, MI

Margaret May Cloud
b. 1846 Mays Landing, NJ
d. 1887 Columbus, OH

Howard F. Thurston   1869-1936
His was the largest traveling magic show of its time, requiring eight
entire train cars to transport.

A resource: *The Last
Greatest Magician in
the World,* by Jim
Steinmeyer (2012)

The Crowley Family Tree
(An exclusive of your humble guide and confidant)

FAMILY NAMES:
Ashby, Bishop, Burgess, Burrell, Carnegie, Chaytor, Hill, Kelly, Lean, Lucas, Shumway, Sparrow, Thrupp, . . .

Drivers come from Cheshire, their surname derived from Norman De Rivers. Pursehouses descend from William de Perci of Stafford (1086).

The first recorded spelling of Bishop anywhere in the world is believed to be Lefwinus Bissop, dated 1166, in the Pipe Rolls of Nottingham.

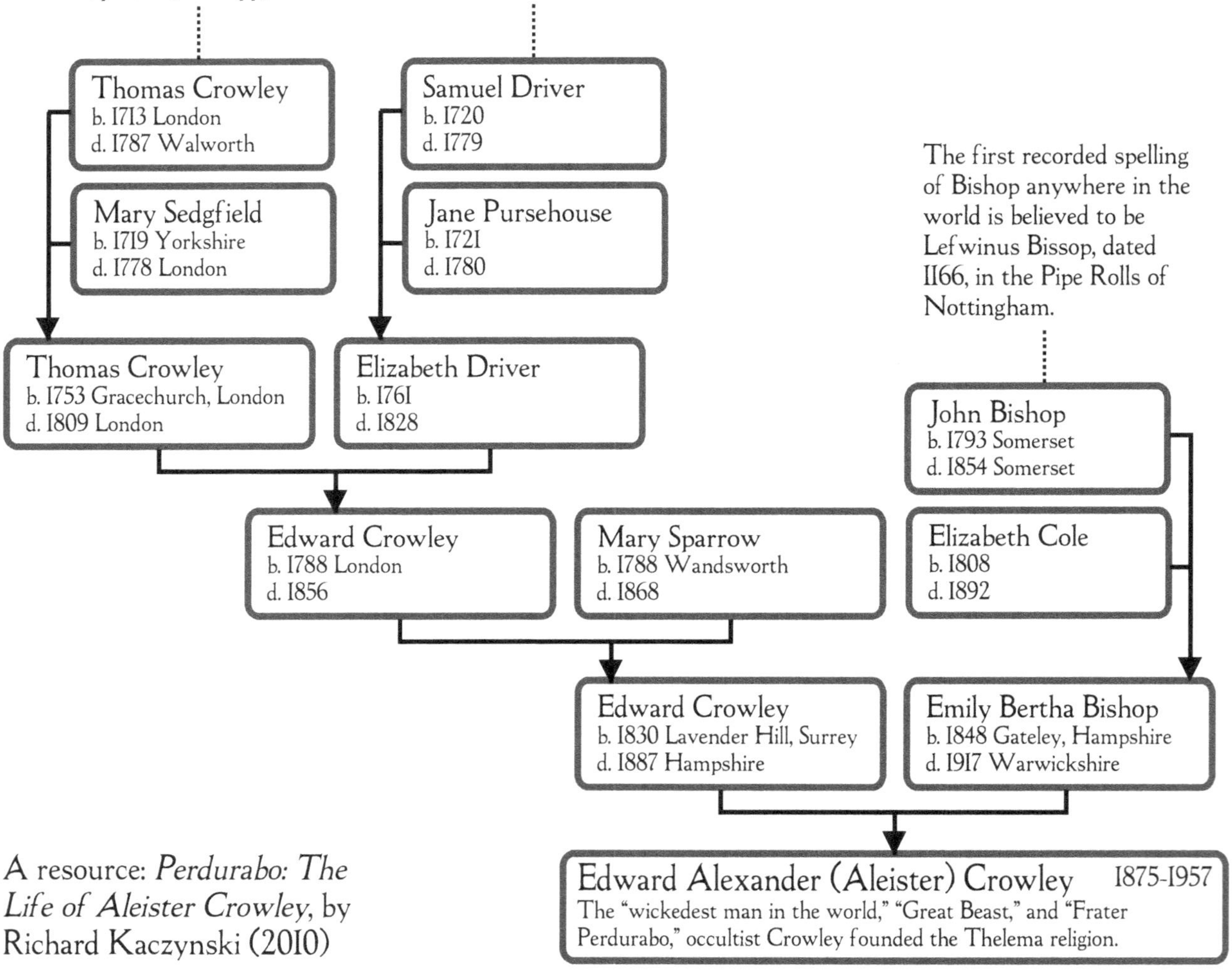

Thomas Crowley
b. 1713 London
d. 1787 Walworth

Mary Sedgfield
b. 1719 Yorkshire
d. 1778 London

Samuel Driver
b. 1720
d. 1779

Jane Pursehouse
b. 1721
d. 1780

Thomas Crowley
b. 1753 Gracechurch, London
d. 1809 London

Elizabeth Driver
b. 1761
d. 1828

John Bishop
b. 1793 Somerset
d. 1854 Somerset

Edward Crowley
b. 1788 London
d. 1856

Mary Sparrow
b. 1788 Wandsworth
d. 1868

Elizabeth Cole
b. 1808
d. 1892

Edward Crowley
b. 1830 Lavender Hill, Surrey
d. 1887 Hampshire

Emily Bertha Bishop
b. 1848 Gateley, Hampshire
d. 1917 Warwickshire

A resource: *Perdurabo: The Life of Aleister Crowley,* by Richard Kaczynski (2010)

Edward Alexander (Aleister) Crowley   1875-1957
The "wickedest man in the world," "Great Beast," and "Frater Perdurabo," occultist Crowley founded the Thelema religion.

The Maskelyne Family Tree

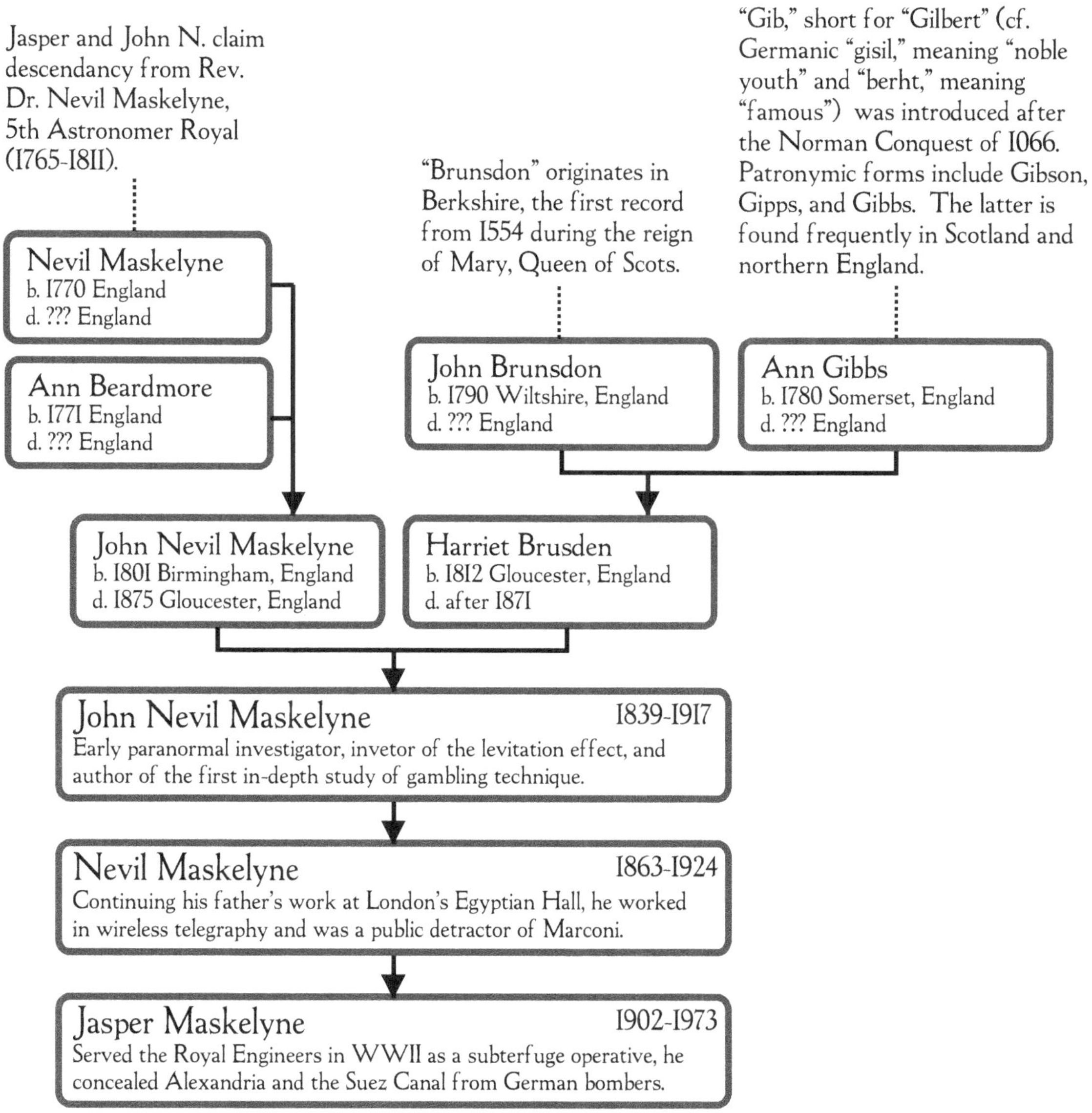

Jasper and John N. claim descendancy from Rev. Dr. Nevil Maskelyne, 5th Astronomer Royal (1765-1811).

"Brunsdon" originates in Berkshire, the first record from 1554 during the reign of Mary, Queen of Scots.

"Gib," short for "Gilbert" (cf. Germanic "gisil," meaning "noble youth" and "berht," meaning "famous") was introduced after the Norman Conquest of 1066. Patronymic forms include Gibson, Gipps, and Gibbs. The latter is found frequently in Scotland and northern England.

Nevil Maskelyne
b. 1770 England
d. ??? England

Ann Beardmore
b. 1771 England
d. ??? England

John Brunsdon
b. 1790 Wiltshire, England
d. ??? England

Ann Gibbs
b. 1780 Somerset, England
d. ??? England

John Nevil Maskelyne
b. 1801 Birmingham, England
d. 1875 Gloucester, England

Harriet Brusden
b. 1812 Gloucester, England
d. after 1871

John Nevil Maskelyne   1839-1917
Early paranormal investigator, invetor of the levitation effect, and author of the first in-depth study of gambling technique.

Nevil Maskelyne   1863-1924
Continuing his father's work at London's Egyptian Hall, he worked in wireless telegraphy and was a public detractor of Marconi.

Jasper Maskelyne   1902-1973
Served the Royal Engineers in WWII as a subterfuge operative, he concealed Alexandria and the Suez Canal from German bombers.

Genealogy is Gray (Magic?)

Foucault: "Genealogy is gray . . . It operates on a field of entangled and confused parchments, on documents that have been scratched over and recopied many times."

How Far Back Dare We Go?

We can forget "the old country." We can forget the Fertile Crescent and the Garden of Eden. The Mayan kings traced their genealogy billions of years *before* the Big Bang. Crucially: "Our ancestors are not only the human inhabitants which make up our family systems. Although for most people veneration of the ancestors is restricted to the human ancestors, it is imperative at this time in history that we include the wider breadth of our relations. Could we not trace our ancestry all the way back to *Australopithecus*? If we are courageous enough we might follow that pedigree even further down what John Moriarty called the

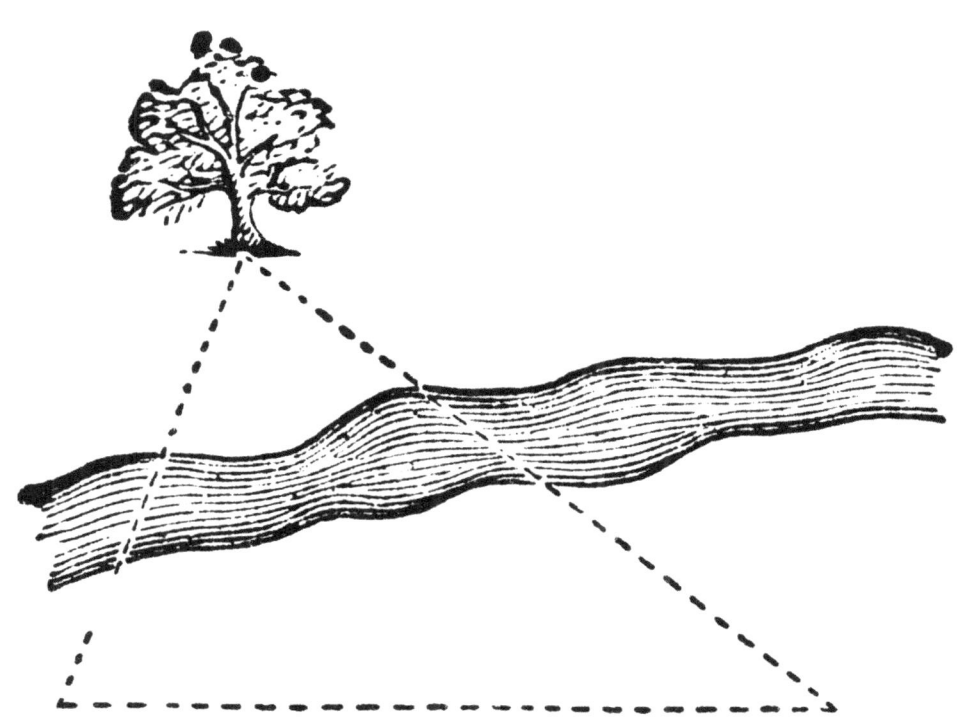

Karmic Canyon: trilobyte, eukaryote, prokaryote, the first form of life to emerge on Earth. Sinking deeper, we might find ourselves in deep relation with the stones, with elemental water itself—even the fire of stars burns in our bodies!" (Jason Kirkey, *The Salmon in the Spring*, 2009).

Astrophysicist Neil DeGrasse Tyson concurs: "The most astounding fact is the knowledge that the atoms that comprise life on Earth, the atoms that make up the human body, are traceable to the crucibles that cooked light elements into heavy elements in their core under extreme temperatures and pressures. These stars, the high-mass ones among them, went unstable in their later years; they collapsed and then exploded, scattering their enriched guts across the galaxy—guts made of carbon, nitrogen, oxygen, and all the fundamental ingredients of life itself. These ingredients became part of the gas clouds that condensed, collapsed, and formed the next generation of solar systems—stars with orbiting planets, and those planets now have the ingredients for life itself. So that when I look up at the night sky, I know that yes, we are in this universe . . . [and] the universe is in us. . . . There's a level of connectivity. That's really what you want in life—you want to feel connected, you want to feel relevant."

Let's dare to trace a family tree at least as far back as one of the twelve worthy goals showcased on the following pages.

Pictured: The history of our ancestry is a road lined with Sphinxes (to paraphrase François Le Lionnais).

The Sea of Microwaves

"The sea of microwaves that fills the universe, the common ancestor of all things" (Rush W. Dozier Jr.).

Ineliminable Vagueness

"Going all the way back to [one's] first ancestor (and here again there will be ineliminable vagueness)" (Alvin Plantinga).

Protoplasmal Primordial Atomic Globule

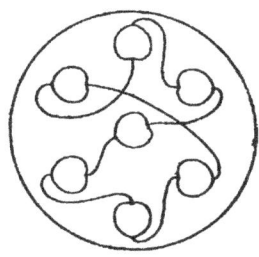

(Gilbert and Sullivan's "Mikado")

A Mayflower

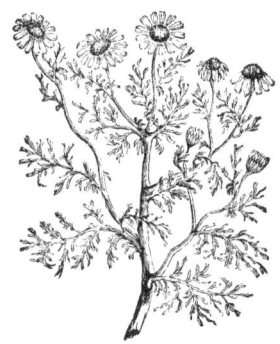

Sail past *the* Mayflower for a May flower.

The Dot

Manly P. Hall foresaw the day "When all peoples can trace their family tree back to the Dot, the form of Nothing" (*The Sacred Magic of the Qabbalah: The Science of Divine Names*, 1923).

Amoeba

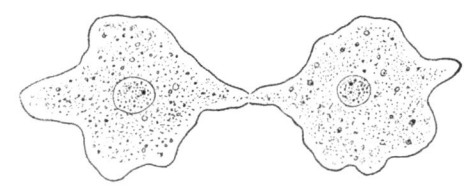

"We can all claim an unbroken chain of successful ancestors all the way back to the first single-celled organism" (Richard Dawkins).

Last Universal Common Ancestor

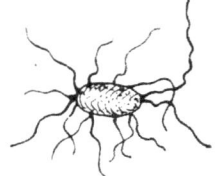

LUCA is the thermophilic bacterium (d. 4 billion BCE) whose DNA all living beings share.

Molecular Cloud

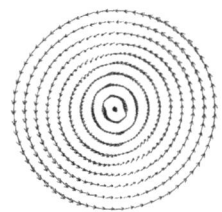

"All the way back to the molecular cloud from which the Solar System was born" (Michael D. Papagiannis).

The Primal Creatrix

Sarcopterygian

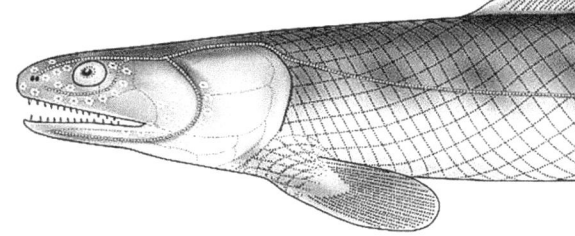

This predatory fish with electrosensors (d. 500 million BCE), is said to be mother to all creatures with a backbone.

Virtrubian Man

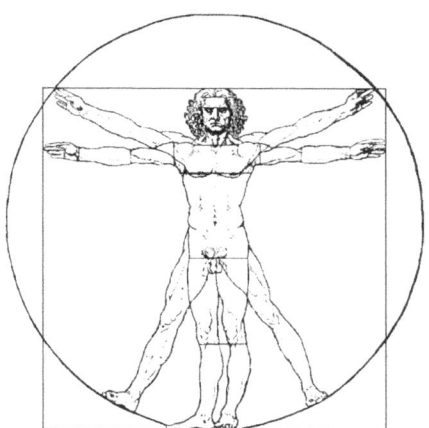

P.T. Barnum's Monkey-headed Fish-bodied Feejee Mermaid

Why not?

Genealogy is a Secret History of Kept Secrets

We are unknown to ourselves, and for a good reason.
—Nietzsche

Genealogy has an axiom: "History never effaces what it buries; it always keeps within itself the secret of whatever it encrypts, the secret of its secret. This is a secret history of kept secrets" (Jacques Derrida).

Pictured: Genius guarding the secret of the tomb.

The First Secret of Genealogy: Fiction Can Be Perfectly Correct

On our eternal quest for intellectual, spiritual, and aesthetic ennoblement, we recall that the burial tablets of initiates into the Ancient Greek mystery cults sport claims of divine lineage. One having been struck by lightning, for example, proved a connection to Zeus. This "ritual genealogy" replaced traditional family lines so as to determine one's place in the cosmos, unhindered by ordinary distinctions of gender, family, or clan (Radcliffe G. Edmonds, "Who Are You? Mythic Narrative and Identity in the 'Orphic' Gold Tablets," *Mystic Cults in Magna Graecia*, 2009).

Verily: "If the only purpose of genealogy were biological ancestry, then the surname should follow the mother's line, because, as any genealogist will tell you, the father is only ever the presumptive parent, whereas the mother is almost always the genetic one." (John Seabrook, *Flash of Genius*, 2008).

Pictured: The branches of Zeus' family tree embrace disparate individuals who have been struck by lightning.

Crucially: A family tree may, at a certain junction, become fictitious but may yet be "perfectly correct according to the logic of the myth" (E. V., "A Study in Shamanism," *The Theosophist*, May 1962, p. 123).

We remember: all truths are fuzzy. Documentary evidence is itself riddled with lies, omissions, and human errors. On census forms, dates are commonly estimated, names are misspelled, and children may be left out. On military enlistment forms, ages are sometimes adjusted (as when someone is legally too young to serve). On marriage certificates, a woman's maiden name is all-too often omitted. On immigration forms, name spellings are often modified. Ship passage logs are often difficult to read and are mistranscribed by indexers. Misdirection abounds.

Pictured: ? ? ?

The Second Secret of Genealogy: All Stories Are True

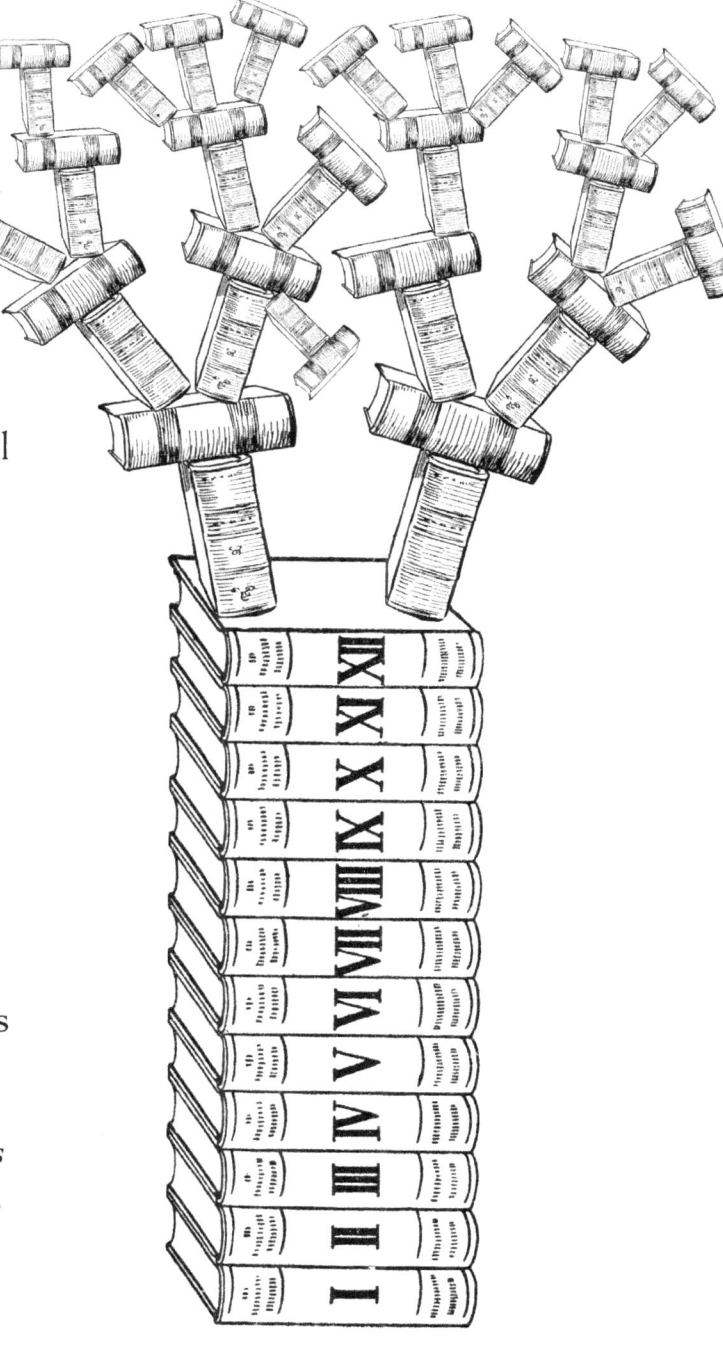

Foucault's "matrix of intersecting lines" is naturally composed of story lines. We recall an African saying that all stories are true. John Edgar Wideman: "When you get right down to it, *knowing* the fact that all stories are true is as much a place to begin as a conclusion, because it doesn't remove the necessity for sorting through the evidence–of working through the stories. What I like about it in particular is that it decentralizes the truth–it fragments the truth. It puts truth in the light of multiplicity, of voices as a kind of construct that you can't arrive at unless you do have a mosaic of voices" (*Conversations with John Edgar Wideman*, 1998).

The Third Secret of Genealogy:
It's a *Means* to Make Historical Truth

We realize that genealogy is counterintuitively more about the present than the past. Nietzsche offered genealogy as "a means to *make* the truths of history in order to meet certain political, social, or cultural needs in the present and for the future. The value of genealogy, therefore, lies in its utility in the present" (Edmund E. Jacobitti, *Composing Useful Pasts*, 2000).

Importantly, Jacobitti notes that "the enhancement of life is the most important criterion governing genealogical practice. In this regard there are no 'correct' interpretations; rather, there are those that either enhance or diminish life. The task of the historian, therefore, is to produce an interpretation, something we can characterize as a *poetic* act, which organizes different perspectives while at the same time employing philological rigor in pursuit of making a truth that will promote the life of the present culture."

The Fourth Secret of Genealogy: It's Bound to Magic

Ancestral spirits, the magical predecessors of the magician. —Bronislaw Malinowski, *The Language of Gardens: An Ethnographic Theory of the Magical Word* (1935)

People like us, who believe in physics, know that the distinction between past, present, and future is only a stubbornly persistent illusion. —Albert Einstein

The bond between genealogy and magic goes way back. Origen, the 3rd century theologian, noted that Egyptian practitioners of magic used the Hebrew names of patriarchs—Abraham, Isaac, and Jacob—to confer power to exorcism recipes (John Granger Cook, *The Interpretation of the Old Testament in Greco-Roman Paganism*, 2004, pp. 103, 109).

The Fifth Secret of Genealogy:
It Produces a Secret Garden

Nietzsche: "Out of my answers there grew new questions, inquiries, conjectures, probabilities—until at length I had a country of my own, a soil of my own, an entire discrete, thriving, flourishing world, like a secret garden the existence of which no one suspected." Wendy Brown explains: "This secret garden is what genealogy intends to produce: this other way of conceiving the familiar, this radical displacement of the lay of the land through which we think we perceive ourselves, our problems, our imperatives. Genealogy promises a worldview that is differently populated and oriented than the one in which we are steeped" (*Politics Out of History*, 2001).

Pictured: The Fairy of Paradise with a star in her hair, from Hans Christian Andersen's "The Garden of Paradise."

The Sixth Secret of Genealogy: It Holds the Secret of the Ages

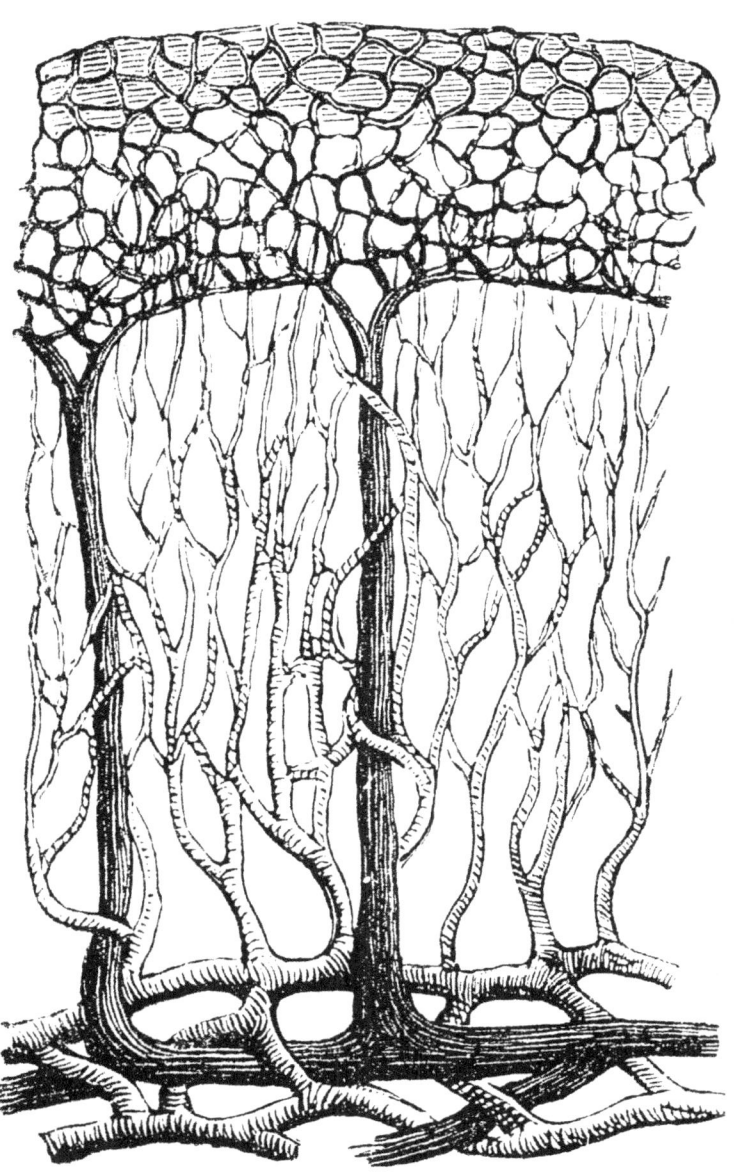

Louise Tracy: "The blood of man holds the secret of the ages; through his veins runs the generations; he is the reincarnation of thousands that have left their earthly immortality in him" (*The Connecticut Magazine*, 1908).

Henry Louis Gates: "The secret of genealogy is that every family story, no matter how seemingly insignificant, and the name and identity of each of our ancestors, no matter how seemingly unremarkable her or his life, contain an abundance of revelations, both about them and about ourselves" (*Faces of America*, 2010).

Pictured: blood vessels branching very like a family tree.

The 7th Secret of Genealogy: Descend Out of Yourself

Stephen J. Pfohl reveals the seventh secret of genealogy: "you must risk descending (out of) yourselves" (*Death at the Parasite Cafe*). Let's allow that thought to simmer in the back of the mind as we gather knowledge to serve as the material upon which to build our grand interpretation of nature.

Branching Pointers

Why It's Not Better Just to Make It All Up

1. The truth is stranger than fiction: We'll stumble upon some bizarre tidbit, unlikely ancedote, or improbable connection that we could never have manufactured.
2. If we reasonably believe our advertised heritage to be genuine, we'll better "sell" that truth to our audience.
3. Genuine genealogical research is a poetic act that enhances life (as per Nietzsche).
4. It's simply more fun.

How to Circumvent Limitations of Family Tree Software

Often we may want to make connections between people other than marriages, such as close alliances, affinities, and namesakes. In your humble guide and confidant's case, family lore records that a great-grandfather was named after fairy tale author Frank Stockton, of *The Lady or the Tiger* fame; to record this information in the family tree,

we identify Stockton as a "partner" of the great-grandfather, with a note at the "Partnership/Family" level explaining the nature of the unique relationship. When some nodes of a descendancy are unknown, it is useful to simply assign the descendant as a "child" of the ancestor and denote the relationship as a "stepchild." This typically has the benefit of being notated with a dotted line in diagrams, which serves as a quick visual indicator that certain steps in the descendancy are pending.

Capitalize on Existing Data Mines

On our quest for balance through aggrandizement, Ancestry.com offers a warehouse of records (censuses, immigration forms, military records, and birth/death certificates), heavily indexed, and surely the most widely used, so we can piggyback off other users' public family trees. Note that while this database is ever-growing, it is heavily focused on the 19th century.

Graft Your Family Tree to a Massive Trunk

Perhaps the best-realized "global family tree" is Geni.com, which constantly seeks to reconcile the disparate work of all users. Once our personal family tree is big enough, Geni is best at connecting us to famous personages.

Flesh Out Ancestral Stories

As we Google every name and date we encounter in our research, we inevitably find tidbits on message boards (like RootsWeb), biographical sketches and media (Wikipedia is good for historical figures), published genealogies, and books related to our relatives (such as Margaret Campbell's profile of Elizabeth of York, *The Tudor Rose: The Story of the Queen Who United a Kingdom and Birthed a Dynasty*).

> The past is not dead. In fact, it's not even past.
> —William Faulkner

Visualize and Organize

We eschew the limitations of traditional paper charts in favor of software. MacFamilyTree, for example, offers a simple interface to collect a virtual scrapbook of anecdotes, images, documents, timelines, and maps. Plus, it offers exhaustive reporting capabilities (with a variety of chart styles) for our permanent records.

Overcoming Research Roadblocks

Even worse than stumbling upon a reprehensible ancestor is running into a seemingly impassable wall that stops a traced line in its tracks. However, because genealogical research is an organic, distributed pursuit, simply waiting a few days and reopening our investigation (possibly from a different angle) will more often than not prove fruitful. "That's the secret of genealogy: experience and persistence. Because if you ever find something in a certain way, you remember to look there again the next time you think you have come to a dead end. By keeping everlastingly at it, you pick up new ways of doing things" (Graham Landrum, *The Famous Dar Murder Mystery*, 2011).

We remember: "In the ancient Mediterranean, Northern Germany and Celtic Europe, the oak was a magical ancestor tree, and everything associated with it, the squirrels, the birds, the bees that live in it, and its acorns were equally magical" (Ronnie Lessem & Alexander Schieffer, *Transformation Management*, 2009).

As a rule, we don't get hung up on any one outcome or spend too much time in search of any one document; we can't predict our leads.

How to "Cheat" and Work Backwards from a Glamorous Ancestor with Whom We *Hope* to Connect

We walk the published family trees of famous or notorious personages, forwards and backwards, simply scanning for family names we recognize. Frequently, walking from those nodes we will encounter a common ancestor, allowing us to formally trace connections (however obtuse). Note that "multi-tasking" is requisite for this approach, as we find ourselves walking multiple trees simultaneously, pinpointing connections in much the same way as finding stars to complete a constellation. In your humble guide and confidant's philosophy, genealogical research is fueled by instinct informing intention; as Tony Buzan puts it, "Creativity is, in a sense, future memory." Put another way, perhaps we wouldn't be exploring a particular connection if we didn't already "intuit" we'd find it.

For Extra Glamor, Connect with Folks Who Have Already Established Legendary, Mythic, or Deified Ancestry

People like to say they're descended from the gods, of course. But how many of us are there, really?
—Bernard Evslin, *Heroes, Gods and Monsters of the Greek Myths* (1984)

🌿 Delve deeply enough into Celtic ancestry, for example, and you're guaranteed to find fairy connections and deified lineage (approximately 50 to 60 generations back).

For example, your humble guide and confidant traced his Conley lineage back to the fairy forts of Ireland—veritable treasure troves of lore. We remember: even a fairy relationship by marriage can be charted on a family tree.

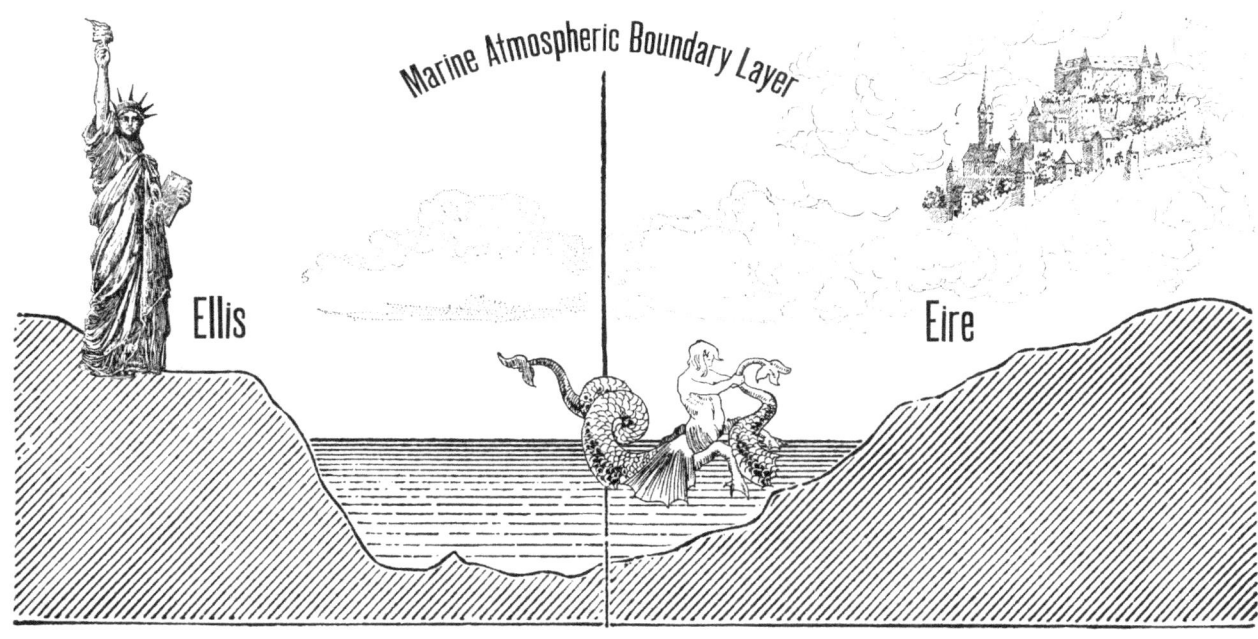

Ellis

Marine Atmospheric Boundary Layer

Eire

> Plato's father traced his ancestry to the sea god Poseidon, while Plato's mother traced hers to the archon Dropides.

> Cyrus of Persia traced his ancestry back to the mythical King Achaemenes.

> The Hapsburgs of Austria traced their ancestry back to the Egyptian fertility god Osiris.

> Julius Caesar descended from the goddess of love, Venus.

> The Scandinavian kings traced their ancestry to the fertility god Freyr in the guise of Ing or Yngvi.

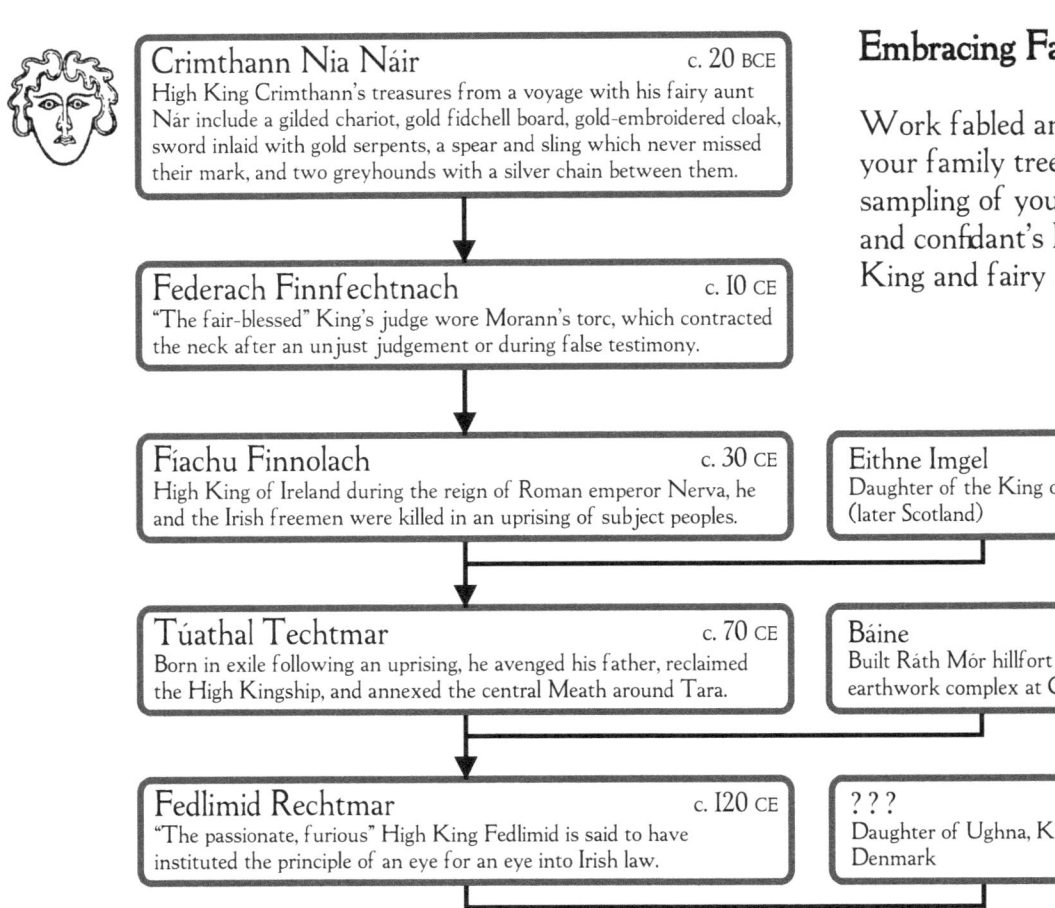

Crimthann Nia Náir · c. 20 BCE
High King Crimthann's treasures from a voyage with his fairy aunt Nár include a gilded chariot, gold fidchell board, gold-embroidered cloak, sword inlaid with gold serpents, a spear and sling which never missed their mark, and two greyhounds with a silver chain between them.

Federach Finnfechtnach · c. 10 CE
"The fair-blessed" King's judge wore Morann's torc, which contracted the neck after an unjust judgement or during false testimony.

Fíachu Finnolach · c. 30 CE
High King of Ireland during the reign of Roman emperor Nerva, he and the Irish freemen were killed in an uprising of subject peoples.

Eithne Imgel
Daughter of the King of Alba (later Scotland)

Túathal Techtmar · c. 70 CE
Born in exile following an uprising, he avenged his father, reclaimed the High Kingship, and annexed the central Meath around Tara.

Báine
Built Ráth Mór hillfort in the earthwork complex at Clogher

Fedlimid Rechtmar · c. 120 CE
"The passionate, furious" High King Fedlimid is said to have instituted the principle of an eye for an eye into Irish law.

? ? ?
Daughter of Ughna, King of Denmark

Conn Cétchathach · c. 150 CE
The five roads to Tara were made visible upon the birth of High King Conn "of the Hundred Battles," who made the coronation stone of Lia Fáil roar beneath his feet.

Eithne Táebfada
Daughter of Cathair Mór and descendant of Mug Corb

Connla Cétchathach · c. 180 CE
Connla fell in love with a fairy woman from Mag Mell, and went with her to her otherworld home in her crystal boat.

Embracing Fairy Heritage

Work fabled anecdotes into your family tree, as in this sampling of your humble guide and confidant's Irish High King and fairy ancestors.

- The highest Hindu caste, the Brahmins, trace their ancestry to the god of ultimate reality, Brahma.

- Emperor Wang Mang traced his ancestry back to the legendary Yellow Emperor, lord of the underworld.

- Marcus Antonius traced his ancestry to the god Hercules, as did Hippocrates before him.

- The Ptolemies claimed to be descended from the god of wine, Bacchus.

- The Tongan chiefs trace their ancestry to the sky god Tangaloa.

- The emperors of Japan traced their ancestry to the goddess of the sun, Amaterasu.

- Galba traced his ancestry back to Jupiter on his father's side.

- All of the royal families (except Essex) go back to the Scandinavian all-father god Odin.

- The Navajo people trace their ancestry to the goddess Changing Woman.

- The Shahs of Kathmandu claimed to be descended from the preserver god Vishnu.

- Augustus traced his ancestry back to the mythical hero and founder of Rome, Aeneas.

- The Yoruba people trace their ancestry to the god of thunder, Shango.

- Genghis Khan traced his ancestry back to the lunar deity.

- Clovis of the Franks traced his ancestry back to the mythical hero Merovius.

- and so on . . .

Deifed Ancestry Courtesy of Odin, the Great Magician
(An exclusive of your humble guide and confidant)

Odin (Roman, Othimus)
By his wife Frea, or Frigga, he had six sons, the fifth of whom was:

↓

Beldig, or Baldar

↓

Brandius, or Brando

↓

Froodigarius, or Froethgar

↓

Wigga

↓

Gewesius, or Gewisch

↓

Effa, or Esta

↓

Effa (the second)

↓

Elesius

Cerdic
Reigned 33 years as the First King of the West Saxons.

↓

Kenric, or Cynric   d. 593
Succeeded as the Second King of the West Saxons to reign for 26 years.

↓

Cheaulin   d. 584
Reigned 32 years until dethroned by his nephew and banished to die in exile.

↓

Cuthwin

↓

Cuth

↓

Chelwold

↓

Kenred

Ingild

Eoppa

Easa

Alkmund, or Aethelmund

Ecgberht, or Egbert   769-839
Claimed the throne of Wessex in 802
after coming of age in exile.

Aethelwulf   795-858
"Noble Wolf" was King of Wessex
from 839 until death. Conquered Kent.

Alfred the Great   849-899
First King of the Anglo-Saxons,
defended against the Viking conquest.

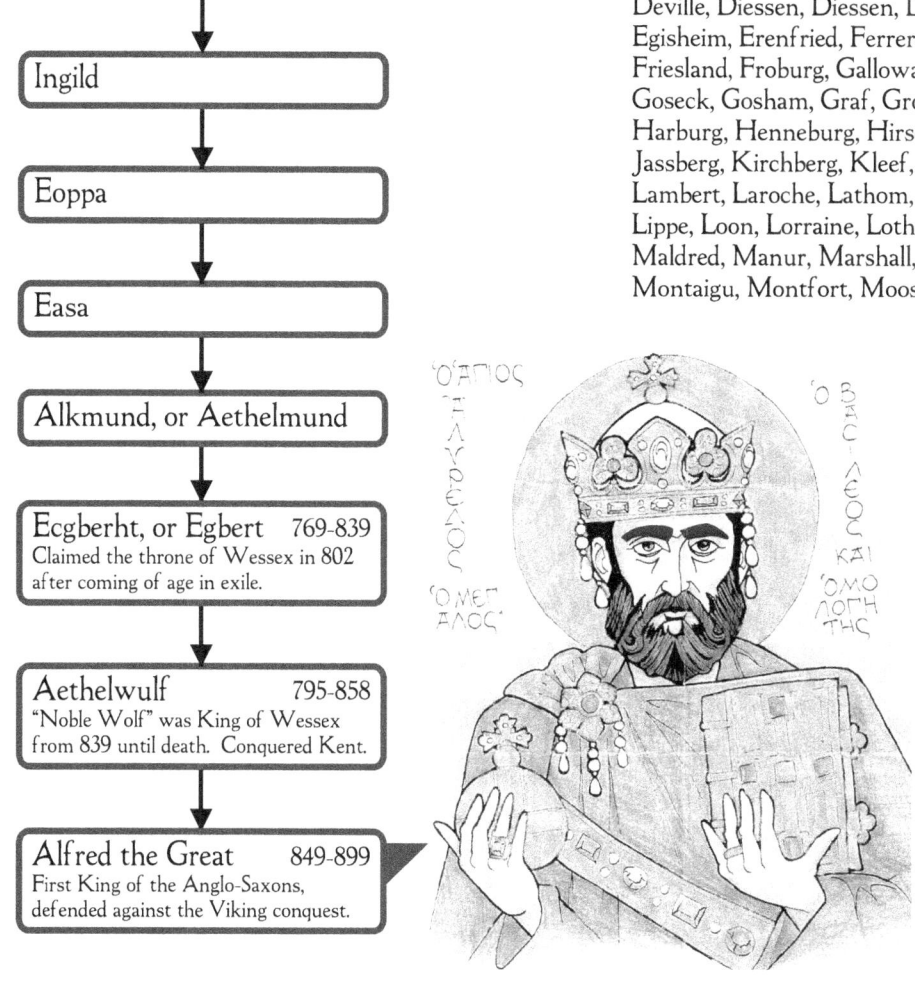

DESCENDANT FAMILY NAMES:
Acahim, Achalm, Adelin, Admont, Albini, Allerdale,
Amiens, Argengau, Armagnac, Arnsberg, Baldwin,
Bamberg, Bayern, Beauclerc, Beaumont, Bec, Berg, Bethune,
Blois, Bocqueville, Bohun, Boulogne, Bourgogne, Brionne,
Broyes, Brus, Buren, Burgundy, Calw, Carlyle, Carolingien,
Chiemgau, Cliveden, Coluim, Courcy, Crequy, Crispin,
Dachau, Dagsburg, Dauphin, Deutz, Devere, Devereux,
Deville, Diessen, Diessen, Diest, Dreux, Dunbar, Durbury,
Egisheim, Erenfried, Ferrers, Flamens, Fleming, Freising,
Friesland, Froburg, Galloway, Gammertingen, Gant, Gent,
Goseck, Gosham, Graf, Gronsveld, Guines, Hainaut,
Harburg, Henneburg, Hirscher, Holland, Hughes, Itter,
Jassberg, Kirchberg, Kleef, Konstanz, Kuckenburg, Lacy,
Lambert, Laroche, Lathom, Lestrange, Leuven, Lindsey,
Lippe, Loon, Lorraine, Lothringen, Louvaine, Ludowinger,
Maldred, Manur, Marshall, Meissen, Merseburg, Mery,
Montaigu, Montfort, Moosburg, Mousson, Munster,
Namur, Neumark, Neville,
Northeim, Osterreich,
Passau, Peteghem, Pfullingen,
Pontheiu, Regensburg,
Reichenbach, Rollancourt,
Rott, Roucy, Sachsen,
Sangerhausen, Saulafeld,
Schannis, Schauenburg,
Schwaben, Schweinfurt,
Sinclair, Smolensk, Speyer,
Speyer, Springer, St.
Martin, Stade, Sudeley,
Talbot, Tangry, Thanning,
Thuringen, Tracy, Tyrol,
Urach, Utrecht, Vaudemont,
Veldenz, Venables, Verdun,
Walbeck, Warren, Warwick,
Wasserburg, Weimar,
Welfen, Wettin, Windberg,
Wittelsbach, Wolfratshausen,
Zurich, Zutphen, . . .

We remember the Emperor Julian's proclamation: "We are all descended from the gods" ("Fragment of a Letter to a Priest"). Yet: "not all have the same relationship with the Gods. In this way, we know that different races must seek linkage with the Gods in different ways, through different traditions, thus interpreting the Gods differently, seeing them in different manifestations" (Robert Blumetti, *Vril: The Life Force of the Gods*, 2010).

In Matters of Contested Identity, Relate Yourself to Each and Every Contender

For example, literary scholars have yet to conclusively prove the identity of the great magician of words known as Shakespeare. There are 79 candidates for authorship, and your humble guide and confidant is joyfully tracing his relation to each and every one of them so as to definitively claim consanguinity. Here's the list of candidates, for those playing along at home:

❧ Alexander, William (1568-1640), 1st Earl of Stirling.

❧ Andrewes, Lancelot (1555-1626), Bishop of Winchester.

❧ Bacon, Anthony (1558-1601), statesman, spy.

❧ Bacon, Francis (1561-1626), lawyer, scholar, essayist.

❧ Barnes, Barnabe (1571-1609), poet, playwright.

❧ Barnfield, Richard (1574-1620), poet.

❧ Bernard, Sir John (1605-1674), husband of Shakespeare's supposed granddaughter.

❧ Blount, Charles (1563-1606), 8th Baron Mountjoy and 1st Earl of Devonshire.

❧ Bodley, Rev. Miles (ca. 1553- ca. 1611), Bible scholar.

❧ Bodley, Sir Thomas (1545-1613), diplomat, scholar.

- Burbage, Richard (1567-1619), actor.

- Burton, Robert (1577-1640), scholar.

- Butts, William (d. 1583), patron of literature.

- Campion, Edmund (1540-1581), poet.

- Cecil, Robert (1563-1612), 1st Earl of Salisbury, statesman.

- Chettle, Henry (1560-1607), playwright, polemicist.

- Daniel, Samuel (1562-1619), poet, historian.

- de Cervantes, Miguel (1547-1616), Spanish novelist, poet, and playwright.

- de Vere, Edward (1550-1604), 17th Earl of Oxford.

- Dekker, Thomas (1572-1632), playwright.

- Devereux, Robert (Essex) (1566-1601), 2nd Earl of Essex.

- Devereux, Walter (c.1541-1576), 1st Earl of Essex.

- Donne, John (1572-1631), poet, Dean of St Paul's Cathedral.

- Drake, Sir Francis (1540-1596), naval commander, adventurer.

- Drayton, Michael (1563-1631), playwright.

- Dyer, Sir Edward (1543-1607), courtier, poet.

- Ferrers, Henry (1549-1633), Warwickshire antiquary.

Fletcher, John (1579-1625), playwright.

Florio, John (1554-1625), linguist.

Florio, Michelangelo (1515-1572), protestant evangelist and scholar.

Greene, Robert (1558-1592), playwright, polemicist.

Greville, Fulke (1554-1628) 1st Baron Brooke.

Griffin, Bartholomew (d. 1602), poet.

Hastings, William. Supposed son of Queen Elizabeth.

Hathaway, Anne (1555/6-1623), Shakespeare's supposed wife.

Herbert, William (1580-1630), 3rd Earl of Pembroke.

Heywood, Thomas (1574-1641), playwright.

The Jesuits. See Harold Johnson's Did the Jesuits Write 'Shakespeare'? (1916).

Jonson, Ben (1572-1637), playwright, poet.

Kyd, Thomas (1558-1594), playwright.

Lanier, Emilia (1569-1645), poet.

Lodge, Thomas (1557-1625), playwright.

Lyly, John (1554-1606), playwright, prose stylist.

Manners, Elizabeth Sidney (d. 1615), Countess of Rutland.

Manners, Roger (1576-1612), 5th Earl of Rutland.

Marlowe, Christopher (1564-1593), playwright.

Mathew, Sir Tobie (1577-1655), courtier, Catholic priest.

Middleton, Thomas (1580-1627), playwright.

More, Sir Thomas (1478-1535), Lord Chancellor of England and Saint of the Catholic Church.

Munday, Anthony (1560-1633), dramatist.

Nashe, Thomas (1567-1601), poet, polemicist.

Neville, Henry (1564-1615) politician and courtier.

North, Thomas (1535-1604), translator of Plutarch.

Nugent, William (1550-1625), Irish rebel.

Paget, Henry (d. 1568), 2nd Baron Paget.

Peele, George (1556-1596), playwright.

Pierce, William (1561-1674), claimed writer.

Porter, Henry (fl. c. 1596-99), playwright.

Raleigh, Sir Walter (1554-1618), courtier, poet.

The Rosicrucians.

Sackville, Thomas (1536-1608), Lord Buckhurst, 1st Earl of Dorset.

Shirley, Sir Anthony (c.1565-1635), soldier, sailor, adventurer.

Sidney Herbert, Mary (1561-1621), Countess of Pembroke. See Robin Williams' *Sweet Swan of Avon: Did a Woman Write Shakespeare?* (2006)

Sidney, Sir Philip (1554-1586), poet, soldier, courtier.

Smith, Wentworth (1571 - c.1623), playwright.

Spenser, Edmund (1552-1599), poet.

Stanley, William, 6th Earl of Derby (1561-1642).

Stuart, James, King of England (1566-1625).

Stuart, Mary (1542-1587), Queen of Scots.

Tudor, Elizabeth (1533-1603), Queen of England.

Warner, William (c.1558-1609), poet.

Watson, Thomas (1555-1592), poet.

Webster, John (c.1580-c.1625), playwright.

Whateley, Anne (c.1561-c.1600), Shakespeare's supposed first fiancée.

Wilson, Robert (1572-1600), playwright.

Wolsey, Thomas (c.1473-1530) Cardinal of England.

Wotton, Sir Henry (1568-1639), scholar, diplomat.

Wriothesley, Henry (1573-1624), 3rd Earl of Southampton.

Zubayr bin William, Shaykh ("Sheik Zubayr").

Make a Show Out of It

We can follow the example of writer/performer David Drake, who traced his family history back to Vlad Dracula and not only presented his research at the World Dracula Congress in Transylvania but also wrote and performed a one-man show about his archetypal identity quest (doing the voices of the colorful people he met along the way).

A Resource

By magician Arthur Kurzweil: *From Generation to Generation: How to Trace Your Jewish Genealogy and Family History* (Jossey-Bass, 2004).

Don't think that by writing to the National Archives . . . some magician is going to produce a family tree for you. No one can provide you with a family tree except you.
–Angus Baxter, *In Search of Your Roots*, 1991

www.ingramcontent.com/pod-product-compliance
Lightning Source LLC
Chambersburg PA
CBHW082152290526
45794CB00008B/3257